·THE·
SUPER MOM
Cookbook

30 RECIPES FOR THE MOM ON THE GO

THE SUPER MOM Cookbook

30 RECIPES FOR THE MOM ON THE GO

Bacon & Cheese Jalapeño Boats

Starters

Italian Stuffed Portobello Mushrooms

Ingredients:

4 large Portobello Mushrooms

2 tbsp. Olive Oil

¼ cup Breadcrumbs

1 Garlic Clove, minced

½ tsp. Sea Salt

½ tsp. Black Pepper

1 tsp. Italian Seasoning

1 tbsp. Tamari

½ cup Mozzarella Cheese, shredded

¼ cup Walnuts, finely chopped

½ Sweet Onion, chopped

¼ cup Vegetable Broth

1 Lemon

2 tbsp. Fresh Parsley, chopped

Instructions:

1. To begin, preheat the oven to 350°F. Clean the mushrooms and dry with a paper towel. Remove the stems and dice them, set aside. In a large skillet over medium-high heat, heat the olive oil. Add the garlic, onions, and mushroom stems and sauté for 2-3 minutes.

2. Add in the juice of one lemon, breadcrumbs, sea salt, black pepper, Italian seasoning, Tamari, and walnuts. Add the broth on top and reduce to medium heat, cook until most of the liquid is dissolved, stirring occasionally.

3. Carefully, one mushroom cap at a time, take the mushroom and spoon the skillet mixture into it until all four mushrooms are evenly filled. Place on a non-stick baking sheet, filling side up. Top with mozzarella cheese and bake for 18-20 minutes.

4. Plate and garnish with parsley, enjoy!

Chicken Skewers with Tzatziki Sauce

Ingredients:

4 (6 oz.) Chicken Breast Fillets

8-10 Wooden Skewers

4 Garlic Cloves, minced

2 Lemons

¼ cup Red Wine Vinegar

⅓ cup Grapeseed Oil

1 tbsp. Thyme

1 tbsp. Oregano

2 tbsp. Dill Weed

14 oz. Greek Yogurt

½ English Cucumber, diced

Himalayan Sea Salt and Black Pepper, to taste

Instructions:

1. To begin, cut the chicken into 1-inch pieces and set aside. In a medium bowl, mix the red wine vinegar, grapeseed oil, juice of 1 lemon, garlic, oregano, and thyme. Add the chicken into the bowl and toss until fully coated. Cover and let marinate for at least 1 hour. Preheat oven to 450°F.

2. Once marinated, use the wooden skewers to thread chicken making sure that they are lightly touching. Repeat until all skewers are full and place on baking sheet. Bake for 5 minutes then remove lower heat to 350°F, and flip the skewers. Place back in the oven for 10-12 minutes or until cooked through.

3. While chicken is cooking, prepare your sauce. In a small bowl mix the juice of 1 lemon, greek yogurt, dill, cucumber and a pinch of black pepper. Keep cold until ready to serve.

4. Serve chicken on skewers with the tzatziki sauce and lemon wedges. Enjoy!

Crab Rangoons

Ingredients:

½ lb. Lump Crab Meat

1 pkg. Wonton Wrappers

6–8 oz. Cream Cheese
(room temperature)

2–4 Scallion Stalks, finely sliced

1 tsp. Worcestershire Sauce

Water

1 tsp. Sugar

Sea Salt for taste

Oil for frying

Instructions:

1. To begin, preheat approx. 1 inch of oil to 325°F over medium heat. While preheating, take a small bowl and combine lump crab meat, scallions, cream cheese, sugar and Worcestershire sauce. Mix well.

2. Lay out the wonton wrappers and scoop about 2 tsp. Into the center of each wrapper. Lightly dab the edges with water to fold the opposite corners together to form a pyramid. Wet the tips of the triangle and fold inward to keep them together.

3. Once all wontons are filled, carefully, place the wontons into the oil for 2–4 minutes or until lightly golden brown.

4. Drain on paper towels, serve with sweet chili sauce. Enjoy!

Shrimp Ceviche

Ingredients:

1 lb. raw Shrimp (deveined and peeled)

8 Limes

1 cup Tomato, chopped

½ cup White Onion, chopped

1 Jalapeño, finely diced

½ cup Cilantro, chopped

Sea Salt and Black Pepper

1 tsp. Cayenne

Instructions:

1. To begin, juice 4 limes and combine with the shrimp. Cover and place in refrigerator for 14-16 minutes (depending on the size of shrimp). In a separate bowl, juice the other 4 limes, chopped tomato, onion, jalapeño, cilantro, and cayenne.
2. Check on shrimp, once fully pink, remove from fridge and combine with the rest of the ingredients. Add sea salt and pepper to taste.
3. Transfer ceviche to a glass bowl, serve with tortilla chips and enjoy!

Bacon & Cheese Jalapeño Boats

Instructions:

1. To begin, cut the jalapeños in half, lengthwise and remove the seeds. In a large skillet over medium-high heat, add the bacon and cook until crispy, about 3-5 minutes per side (depending on the thickness). Remove from skillet and place on paper towel to drain excess oil. Once dry, dice the bacon into small pieces.

2. Preheat the oven to 350°F. In a medium bowl, combine the following: 3/4 cup cheddar cheese, cream cheese, garlic powder, 3/4 of the crushed bacon, and sea salt. Mix well until smooth. Arrange the peppers on non-stick baking sheet and begin spooning about ¼ cup into each jalapeño half. Repeat until all jalapeños are filled.

3. Use the remaining ¼ cup of cheddar cheese to top the jalapeños. Bake for 15-20 minutes, until cheese is melted and bubbly. Remove from oven and transfer to serving plate.

4. Garnish with reserved bacon pieces and serve immediately. Enjoy!

Ingredients:

6 Jalapeño Peppers

5 slices Bacon

1 cup Cheddar Cheese, shredded

6 oz. Cream Cheese (room temperature)

½ tsp. Garlic Powder

½ tsp. Sea Salt

Crab Au Gratin Dip

Ingredients:

1 lb. Jumbo Lump Crab Meat
½ Yellow Onion, chopped
2 Garlic Cloves, minced
4 oz. Cream Cheese (room temperature)
3/4 cup Half & Half
1 ½ sticks of Butter, melted
1 cup Cheddar Cheese, shredded
1 cup Gruyére Cheese, shredded
½ tsp. Cayenne Pepper
2 tbsp. Flour
1 tbsp. Lemon Juice
Sea Salt and Black Pepper, to taste

Instructions:

1. To begin, preheat oven to 350°F. In a large skillet over medium-high heat, melt the butter. Add in the garlic and onions and cook, stirring occasionally, until translucent. About 5 minutes. Add in the flour to the skillet and stir, do not let flour brown. About 2 minutes.

2. Add in the half & half, stirring constantly. Stir in the lemon juice, cayenne, salt, and pepper. Keep stirring to create creamy soup thickness. Add water if it becomes too thick, 1 tbsp. at a time. Remove from heat and add in the cheddar cheese, gruyére, and cream cheese. Blend well by folding over until completely melted.

3. Divide the crabmeat among 3-4 oven-proof bowls. Pour the cheese sauce over the crab, evenly. Top with additional cheese or leftover crab.

4. Place in oven and allow to bake for about 13-15 minutes, depending on your bowls. Once bubbly, switch to broil for 4-5 minutes. Remove from oven and serve with bread or chips. Enjoy!

Fiesta Street Corn Dip

Ingredients:

3 cups Sweet Corn

1 ½ tbsp. Olive Oil

⅓ cup Cotija Cheese

2 tsp. fresh Lime Juice

⅓ cup Mayonnaise

⅓ cup Red Onion, diced

⅓ cup Cilantro Leaves, chopped

2 tsp. Paprika or Chili Powder

1 Garlic Clove, minced

Himalayan Sea Salt and Black Pepper, to taste

Instructions:

1. To begin, heat olive oil on medium-high heat. Add the corn and stir occasionally to achieve a slightly charred flavor. Remove from heat. Allow cooling for 5-10 minutes. In a medium bowl, mix the following: corn, mayonnaise, lime juice, garlic, red onion, and paprika together.

2. Add cilantro, Cotija cheese, salt, and pepper to season and lightly toss. Serve in chilled bowl with cilantro to garnish. Serve with warm tortilla chips! Enjoy!

Fried Fish Bites

Ingredients:

1 lb. Cod Fillets (1 in. pieces)
1 Lemon
1 cup Flour
½ tsp. Garlic Powder
½ tsp. Paprika
½ tsp. Parsley
½ cup Milk
1 Egg, beaten
1 cup Panko Breadcrumbs
½ cup Mayo
2 tbsp. Sour Cream
3 tbsp. Sweet Relish
½ tsp. Fresh Dill, chopped
Himalayan Sea Salt and Black Pepper, to taste

Instructions:

1. To begin, preheat the oven to 425°F. In a mixing bowl add the mayo, sour cream, sweet relish, dill, and pepper and mix well. Whisk until smooth, cover and set in the refrigerator.

2. Prepare 3 separate bowls or plates for the following: First bowl, add in the flour, garlic powder, pepper, and salt. The second bowl, mix the beaten egg and milk. The third bowl, add in the panko crumbs and paprika.

3. In that order, dip the fish pieces in flour mixture, then egg, finished with breadcrumbs. Add fish on a non-stick or sprayed baking sheet. Repeat until all fish is covered.

4. Bake for 15-20 minutes, until golden crispy. Flip halfway through. Remove from heat and serve with homemade tartar sauce. Garnish with lemon wedges, parsley and enjoy!

Bacon, Brie & Onion Bites

Ingredients:

French Baguette

6 slices Bacon

1 block of Brie

4 cups Yellow Onions, sliced thinly

1 ½ cups Apple Cider Vinegar

2 tsp. Thyme Leaves

¼ White Wine Vinegar

¼ cup Brown Sugar

1 tsp. Ground Ginger

Himalayan Sea Salt and Pepper, to taste

Instructions:

1. Preheat oven to 350°F. While it preheats, cut the baguette into diagonal slices and place them on a baking sheet. Brush both sides with olive oil, sprinkle black pepper and Himalayan sea salt to season. Bake until golden, 15 to 20 minutes. Remove from heat and allow to cool.

2. While crostinis bake, heat a large saucepan on medium-high heat. Add bacon to pan and cook until lightly crispy. Remove from heat and let cool. Using the excess fat in the pan add in the onions. Lower heat to medium, stir occasionally until onions softened.

3. Chop bacon into ¼ inch pieces and add it into the pan with the onions. Add in the ACV, thyme, a pinch of salt and pepper, brown sugar, and ginger into pan.

4. Leave uncovered and cook until liquid is almost non-existent. Reduce heat to low and allow onions to cook until rich brown color. Add ⅓ cup water if starts to become too dry.

5. Once it reaches the desired color, remove from heat to let cool. Slice brie into thin slices and place on top of crostinis. Top with bacon, onion marmalade, and garnish with fresh thyme. Serve and enjoy!

Fried Calamari

Ingredients:

1 lb. Calamari, cut into rings

1 cup Cornmeal

1 cup Cornstarch

1 cup Milk

1 tbsp. Seafood Seasoning

1 tsp. Cayenne

1 Lemon

Canola Oil, to fry

Himalayan Sea Salt

Parsley, for garnish

Instructions:

1. To begin, clean and cut the calamari into rings. In a container add the calamari, milk and Seafood seasoning to tenderize. Stir and refrigerate overnight.

2. Heat a frying pan of Canola oil on medium-high, until oil reaches a temperature of 350-375°F. In a bowl, combine the cornstarch, cornmeal, salt and cayenne pepper. Remove the calamari from the milk, coat in the cornstarch mixture and fry a few calamari at a time, for about 3-4 minutes, until golden and crispy.

3. Remove calamari from oil, soak off excess oil with paper towel. Add into a serving dish, garnish with lemon wedges and parsley. Serve with marinara and enjoy!

Roasted Eggplant with Lemon-Yogurt and Pomegranate

Main Dishes

Salmon Patties

Ingredients:

1 lb. Wild Salmon (no skin)

⅓ cup Panko Breadcrumbs

6 Hatch Chiles, chopped

½ Red Onion, diced

2 tbsp. Cilantro, chopped

2 tbsp. Olive Oil

1 tbsp. Paprika

½ tsp. Garlic Powder

½ tsp. Cayenne (adjust to taste)

2 tbsp. Grated Parmesan

¼ cup Mayonnaise

Himalayan Sea Salt and Black Pepper, to taste

Instructions:

1. To begin, place salmon chunks in a medium bowl and begin breaking up into smaller pieces using a fork. Once fairly small chunks, add in the hatch chiles, red onion, cilantro, garlic powder, paprika, and cayenne.

2. Mix well, add in the mayo and breadcrumbs until you get a consistency that will hold it together. Form the patties to your desired size and place aside.

3. Heat a medium skillet on medium heat, add olive oil. Place patties about 1 inch apart and let cook, covered for about 6 minutes on each side. Once it is lightly crispy on the exterior, remove from heat.

4. Serve over cabbage, in a burger bun, or as is! Enjoy!

Simple Turkey Tacos

Ingredients:

1 ½ lb. Ground Turkey (Lean)

1 cup Red Onion, diced

2 Garlic Cloves, minced

1 tbsp. Olive Oil

2 tsp. Paprika

1 tsp. Chili Powder

½ tsp. Cinnamon

½ tsp. Black Pepper

½ tsp. Sea Salt

1 tbsp. Tomato Paste

¼ cup Water

6-8 (6-inch) Corn Tortillas

Avocado (optional)

For the Lime Cream Sauce:

¼ cup Sour Cream

3 tbs. Mayonnaise

2 Limes, zest only

1 tbsp. Fresh Lime Juice

Instructions:

1. To begin, heat a medium saucepan over medium-high heat. Add the olive oil, garlic, and red onion. Cook for 2-3 minutes, until fragrant. Add in the ground turkey and cook for 8-10 minutes, stirring throughout.

2. While the turkey cooks, whisk together the sour cream, mayonnaise, rest of the zest, sea salt, and 1 lime juiced in a small bowl. Set aside in a cool place.

3. Add in the tomato paste, water, paprika, chili powder, cinnamon, black pepper, and sea salt. Mix well. Using a separate medium pan, heat over medium-high heat and cook tortillas about 15-30 seconds each side.

4. Scoop the turkey into the tortillas and drizzle with the lime cream sauce. Add avocado if desired. Enjoy!

Roasted Eggplant with Lemon-Yogurt & Pomegranate

Ingredients:

2 Whole Eggplants
½ cup Pomegranate Seeds
1 tsp. Fresh Parsley, chopped
(additional for garnish)
3 Garlic Cloves, minced
½ cup Plain Greek Yogurt
2 tbsp. Walnuts, chopped
2 tbsp. Olive Oil
1 tbsp. Lemon Juice
1 tsp. Lemon Zest
1 tsp. Sea Salt
½ tsp. Onion Powder
½ tsp. Cumin
½ tsp. Black Pepper

Instructions:

1. To begin, carefully, cut the eggplant into 4 slices, lengthwise. Try to keep them all about the same thickness. In a small bowl, mix the following: parsley, garlic, sea salt, onion powder, cumin, and black pepper. Brush 1 tbsp. olive oil on both sides of the eggplant slices then season on both sides.

2. Place them flat on a cast iron skillet, top with foil, then top with another pan so it presses them down. Keep the stacked pans over medium-high heat and allow to roast for about 18-20 minutes, until tender.

3. While the eggplant roasts, combine the lemon juice, lemon zest, greek yogurt and a sprinkle of sea salt in a bowl.

4. Remove from oven and evenly divide among 4 plates. Top each eggplant slice with 1 tbsp. of lemon yogurt mixture, 1 tsp. pomegranate seeds (more if desired) and fresh parsley! Enjoy!

Shrimp Fried Rice

Ingredients:

2 cups Basmati Rice

10-12 Shrimp (deveined, with Tail)

3 Beaten Eggs

3 Scallion Stalks, sliced

2 tbsp. Olive Oil

5 tbsp. Sesame Oil

5 tbsp. Soy Sauce

2 tbsp. Garlic Powder

1 tbsp. Chili Powder

1 tsp. Ginger Powder

1 tbsp. Lemon Juice

⅓ cup Frozen Peas

1 small Yellow Onion, diced

Himalayan Sea Salt, to taste

Instructions:

1. To begin, bring 1 ½ cups of water with a pinch of salt to boil in a medium pot over medium-high heat. Stir in the rice while boiling, reduce heat to medium-low, cover and let simmer until liquid is absorbed 14-18 minutes. Remove from heat and set aside.

2. In a medium bowl, add the sesame oil, soy sauce, lemon juice, garlic, chili powder, ginger, and onion. Mix well.

3. In a large saucepan, heat the oil over medium-high heat. Add the shrimp in an even layer, cooking each side for 2 minutes. Remove shrimp from pan and set aside. Using the same saucepan, add the mixture from the bowl and sauté for 1-2 minutes. Add the frozen peas and egg, stirring. Add the shrimp back in, tossing to ensure they are fully coated.

4. Add in the rice, tossing occasionally for 2-3 minutes. Remove from heat, serve and garnish with scallions. Enjoy!

Skirt Steak with Bleu Cheese Sauce

Ingredients:

1 lb. Skirt Steak

3 Garlic Cloves, minced

1 lb. Asparagus

3 tbsp. Olive Oil

½ cup Dry Red Wine

1 tsp. Chives, chopped

2 tbsp. Shallots, chopped

½ cup Sour Cream

2 oz. (about ½ cup) Bleu Cheese
    Crumbles, room temperature

2 tsp. Sea Salt

1 tsp. Black Pepper

Instructions:

1. To begin, create the marinade. In a baking dish, mix the following: red wine, garlic cloves, 1 tsp. sea salt and black pepper. Mix well then add the skirt steak, flipping to cover. Marinate for at least 2 hours, turning the steak halfway through.

2. Preheat your broiler. Once ready, broil the steak on the closest rack for 4-6 minutes per side. While the steak broils, get your bleu cheese sauce ready!

3. In a saucepan, over medium-high heat add 2 tbsp. olive oil and shallots. Sauté until softened, 1-2 minutes. Add in the white wine, and bring to a simmer until about half of the liquid has evaporated. Add in the sour cream, salt, and pepper. Mix well and slowly stir in the bleu cheese crumbles, stir until smooth.

4. In another skillet over medium-high heat, heat the remaining olive oil. Add in the asparagus, tossing occasionally and cook for 8-10 minutes, until cooked through.

5. Remove skirt steak from oven, transfer to cutting board and cut into ¼ inch pieces. Top with bleu cheese sauce and fresh chives. Serve with asparagus and enjoy!

Salmon Salad with Pomegranate

Ingredients:

8 oz. Salmon Fillet, skin on

8-10 cups Spring Spinach Mix

⅓ cup Canned Mandarin Oranges

¼ cup Pomegranate Seeds

3 tbsp. Olive Oil

1 tbsp. Balsamic Vinegar

1 tbsp. Garlic Powder

Himalayan Sea Salt and Black Pepper, to taste

Instructions:

1. To begin, preheat the oven to 350°F. Place the salmon fillet on a baking sheet, skin-side down. Brush fillet with olive oil, garlic powder, and salt. Place in the oven and let bake for 14-16 minutes, until flaky.

2. In a large salad bowl, create a bed with your spring mix. Add in the mandarin oranges and pomegranate seeds.

3. Using a sharp knife, carefully remove the skin of the salmon and discard. Place the salmon on top of the salad, drizzle with balsamic vinegar and mix well, breaking apart the salmon into bite-size chunks.

4. Evenly distribute the salad among bowls, garnish with extra pomegranate seeds and serve. Enjoy!

Stuffed Chicken Caprese

Ingredients:

4 (6 oz.) Chicken Breast Fillets
⅓ cup Sun-dried Tomato Oil
3 Garlic Cloves, minced
2 Roma Tomatoes, sliced
12-15 Fresh Basil leaves
4 slices Mozzarella Cheese
½ cup Mozzarella Cheese, shredded
2 tsp. Italian Seasoning
⅓ cup Balsamic Vinegar
Himalayan Sea Salt

Instructions:

1. To begin, preheat the oven to 350°F. Take the chicken breasts and cut each into a pocket of about 3/4 of the way through the side being careful not to cut all the way through. Lightly drizzle the sun-dried tomato oil on each chicken fillet, then season with salt, pepper, and the Italian seasoning.

2. In each pocket, fill the chicken with 2 tomato slices, basil leaves, and mozzarella slice. To seal, use 3-4 toothpicks while cooking to keep contents inside the pocket.

3. In a large skillet over medium-high heat, heat 2 tbsp. Sun-dried tomato oil. Add the chicken and cook on each side for 2-3 minutes or until golden. While cooking, in a mixing bowl add the garlic, balsamic vinegar and a touch of salt. Pour around the chicken breasts in the skillet, bring to a simmer while stirring occasionally. Cook for about 2 minutes or until the sauce has thickened.

4. Top the chicken breasts evenly with the shredded mozzarella cheese and transfer the skillet to the oven for 12-15 minutes, or until the chicken is cooked through.

5. Remove from oven and carefully remove the toothpicks. Serve immediately and top with remaining sauce. Garnish with fresh basil and enjoy!

Cedar Plank Salmon

Instructions:

1. To begin, soak the cedar plank in water for at least 45-60 minutes. Spray the plank with oil and preheat the oven to 350°F. Carefully place the plank inside the oven while preheating.

2. Combine the paprika, salt, garlic powder, dried dill, lemon pepper, and the ginger in a small bowl. Place the salmon, skin on the plank. Rub the seasoning onto the salmon and top with a lemon round.

3. Bake for about 10-12 minutes, until salmon is cooked through to medium and flakey. Garnish with fresh parsley atop the lemon and enjoy!

Ingredients:

1 lb. Wild Caught Salmon Fillet, skin on
1 Cedar Plank
1 tbsp. Paprika
1 tsp. Himalayan Sea Salt
1 tsp. Garlic Powder
½ tsp. Dried Dill
1 tbsp. Lemon Pepper
½ tsp. Ginger Powder
1 Lemon
Fresh Dill, for garnish

Lemon Garlic Shrimp Scampi

Ingredients:

1 ½ lb. Large Shrimp, deveined

8 oz. Angel Hair Spaghetti

4 Garlic Cloves, minced

3 Lemons

1 cup Virgin Olive Oil

½ cup Grated Parmesan Cheese

1 cup Fresh Parsley, chopped

Himalayan Sea Salt and Pepper, to taste

Instructions:

1. To begin, zest 2 lemons and add zest into a medium bowl. Toss together with shrimp, ⅓ cup olive oil, parsley, and minced garlic. Set aside to marinate for at least 25 minutes, room temperature.

2. While marinating, bring a large pot of water to boil (add a pinch of sea salt). Once boiling, add spaghetti and cook for about 8-10 minutes, until tender. Remove and drain spaghetti, keeping 1 cup of spaghetti water.

3. While spaghetti cooks, heat a large skillet on medium-high heat and add shrimp to saucepan. Make sure they are all even and turn over after about 2-3 minutes. Once cooked transfer shrimps to a bowl.

4. In a small bowl, combine ½ cup olive oil, lemon juice of 2 lemons and the parmesan cheese. Combine the drained spaghetti and lemon-cheese mixture in the skillet and toss thoroughly. Add a little bit of spaghetti water at a time. Add in the parsley, sea salt, and pepper for taste.

5. Plate evenly and garnish with fresh lemon zest and parmesan cheese. Enjoy!

Fish Tacos with Cabbage Slaw

Ingredients:

1 lb. Cod Fillets
3 Limes
1 tbsp. Paprika
2 tbsp. Ground Cumin
3 Garlic Cloves, minced
¼ cup Soy Sauce, low sodium
¼ cup Fresh Orange Juice
8 (6 in.) Flour Tortillas
1 Avocado
Himalayan Sea Salt and Ground Pepper
2 tbsp. Cilantro, chopped
½ Green Onion, sliced
2 cups Red and Green Cabbage, finely shredded

For the Lime Cream Sauce:

¼ cup Sour Cream
3 tbsp. Mayonnaise
2 Limes, zest only
1 tbsp. Fresh Lime Juice

Instructions:

1. To begin, combine fresh orange juice, ½ of the lime zest, juice of 1 lime, garlic, and soy sauce in a small bowl. Pour into a Ziplock bag and add fish, let marinate for 20–30 minutes in the refrigerator. At this time preheat oven to 425°F.

2. While marinating, whisk together the sour cream, mayonnaise, rest of the zest, sea salt, and 1 lime juiced in a small bowl. Set aside in a cool place.

3. Grab a large bowl and add the 2 cups of shredded cabbage, cilantro, green onion, and red onion. Toss thoroughly and place in the refrigerator until ready to serve.

4. Remove the fish and place on a non-stick baking sheet. Bake for about 10-12 minutes, until the fish is flaky and cooked through. While cooking, heat a large skillet on medium-high and warm each tortilla for 1-2 minutes on each side. Remove from heat and place in a warm towel to keep warm.

5. Transfer the fish to a plate and gently break into pieces with a fork. Divide the fish evenly on the tortillas, top with the cabbage slaw, lime cream sauce, and avocado. Serve and enjoy!

Snickerdoodle Cookies

Desserts

Blueberry Cobbler

Ingredients:

2 pints Fresh Blueberries

2/3 cup Whole Milk

3/4 cup Sugar

1 All-purpose Flour

6 tbsp. Butter (individually cut by tbsp.)

1 tsp. Sea Salt

2 tsp. Baking Powder

1 tsp. Vanilla Extract

1 tsp. Cinnamon

2 tsp. Cornstarch

1 tbsp. Lemon Juice

2 ½ tbsp. Water

Instructions:

1. To begin, preheat the oven to 400°F. In a large cast-iron skillet, over medium-high heat, melt 3 tbsp. butter. Add the following: blueberries, water, cornstarch, lemon juice, cinnamon, and ½ cup sugar. Stir until the cornstarch begins to dissolve.

2. Bring to a boil, then reduce and let simmer for 3-4 minutes. Remove pan from heat, set aside. In a medium mixing bowl, mix the following: remaining sugar, baking powder, flour, and sea salt. Chop up the remaining butter into smaller pieces.

3. Add the tiny butter pieces into the mixing bowl, along with the milk and vanilla extract. Stir until mixture is smooth and well mixed.

4. Pour the mixture on top of the blueberries, smoothing to cover the entire skillet. Bake for 20-22 minutes, until the top, is lightly golden and the blueberries are starting to bubble over. Remove from heat and let cool for 5-8 minutes, spoon mixture onto plates and serve with homemade vanilla ice cream. Enjoy!

Chocolate Croissants

Ingredients:

2 Croissant Dough Sheets, thawed

1 Egg, beaten

1 tbsp. Water

1 lb. Baking Chocolate

2 oz. Milk Chocolate, melted

2 tbsp. All-purpose Flour

¼ cup Butter, melted

Instructions:

1. To begin, preheat the oven to 400°F. Lightly flour the surface and roll out the croissant dough, cutting into triangles. Cut the baking chocolate into 12 even pieces for the filling. Use the melted butter to brush the inside of the croissant, then place a piece of chocolate on each triangle (the widest part).

2. Working from the widest end, roll the dough up to the pointed end and fold. Repeat until all croissants are rolled. In a small bowl, mix the egg and water. Whisk until smooth, then brush over all the croissants.

3. Place the croissants on a greased or non-stick baking sheet, at least 1 inch apart from each other. Bake for 15-17 minutes, until golden crispy.

4. Remove from oven, let cool for 5-8 minutes, while cooling prepare your chocolate. Melt the milk chocolate and transfer to a Ziploc bag. Squeeze into one of the bottom corners of the bag, then cut a tiny corner off to create an opening for the chocolate. Drizzle in your desired pattern on the tops of all croissants. Let sit for 2-3 minutes, then serve. Enjoy with a cup of coffee!

Pumpkin Spice Blondies

Ingredients:

3 cups All-purpose Flour

3/4 cup Pumpkin Puree

1 cup Brown Sugar

1 cup Sugar

1 cup Butter, melted

1 Egg Yolk

1 ½ tsp. Vanilla Extract

1 tsp. Ground Cinnamon

1 tsp. Pumpkin Spice

½ tsp. Nutmeg

3/4 tsp. Sea Salt

¼ tsp. Baking Powder

Pumpkin Seeds (optional, for garnish)

Instructions:

1. To begin, preheat the oven to 350°F. In a medium-sized mixing bowl, whisk the butter, brown sugar, and regular sugar together. Once well combined, add in the egg yolk, pumpkin puree, and vanilla extract. Keep mixing.

2. In a separate mixing bowl, combine the following ingredients: 2 3/4 cups flour, nutmeg, pumpkin spice, salt, and baking powder. Stir in the dry mixture into the pumpkin mixture, keep stirring until well combined.

3. Prepare a non-stick or greased pan, pour in the mixture and even out with a spoon. In a small bowl, mix about 2-3 tbsp. sugar and the cinnamon together. Sprinkle on the entire mixture.

4. Bake for 20-25 minutes. Remove from oven and let cool for at least 5 minutes. Garnish with pumpkin seeds, if desired. Enjoy!

Lemon Poppy Seed Muffins

Ingredients:

3/4 cup Sugar

6 tbsp. Butter, melted

1 Egg

1 cup Flour

¼ cup Sour Cream

1 tsp. Baking Powder

1 tsp. Baking Soda

1 tsp. Lemon Zest

1 ½ tsp. Lemon Juice

1 ½ tbsp. Poppy Seeds

Instructions:

1. To begin, preheat the oven to 375°F. In a large mixing bowl, add the sugar, flour, baking powder, baking soda, and lemon zest, and a tiny pinch of salt. Whisk to combine. In a separate bowl, add the melted butter, egg, sour cream, and lemon juice. Whisk as well.
2. Pour the wet mixture into the dry mixture and mix well. Keep mixing while stirring in the poppy seeds. Line a cupcake pan with muffin cup liners.
3. Using a measuring spoon, add about 3/4 batter into each cup liner until all batter has been used. Bake for 20-25 minutes, or until golden brown. Allow to cool for 5 minutes, then serve. Enjoy!

Mini Donut Bites

Ingredients:

12 oz. Biscuit Dough

½ cup Sugar

⅓ cup Ground Cinnamon

6-8 cups Vegetable Oil

Icing (optional)

Instructions:

1. Heat a large pot over medium-high heat and add the vegetable oil. While the oil heats up, open the biscuit dough and roll out into a sheet.
2. Using scissors or a knife, cut small 1-inch pieces of dough and set aside.
3. Once the oil is hot, drop in 4-6 bite size dough pieces into the oil. Use a strainer to flip and cook evenly, about 1-2 minutes or until golden.
4. Remove from the oil and onto a paper towel. Repeat until all are cooked.
5. While still hot, toss the donut bites in a mixing bowl with the sugar and cinnamon.
6. Transfer to a bowl and serve. Enjoy!

Snickerdoodle Cookies

Ingredients:

3 cups All-purpose Flour
1 ½ cup Sugar
1 cup Butter, melted
1 Large Egg
1 ½ tsp. Vanilla Extract
1 ½ tsp. Ground Cinnamon
1 tsp. Baking Powder
¼ tsp. Sea Salt

Instructions:

1. To begin, preheat the oven to 350°F. In a bowl, mix the following ingredients: Flour, baking powder, and sea salt. In a separate bowl, mix the melted butter and 1 ¼ cup sugar. Once fluffy, add in the egg and vanilla. Continue to mix until well combined.

2. Pour in the flour mixture into the butter mixture, continue stirring. Mixture should be nice and smooth, if it is sticking add in 1 tsp. of flour at a time to fix.

3. On a plate, add the remaining sugar and cinnamon together. Lightly mix and set aside. Using a ¼ cup measuring cup or an ice cream scoop, one at a time take out a scoop of dough and roll into a ball. Then roll the ball in the cinnamon sugar and set aside. Repeat until all cookies are rolled and coated.

4. Place the cookie rolls on a greased baking sheet. Bake for 12-15 minutes, do NOT overcook so that it is still chewy. Remove from heat and allow to cool for a few minutes. Sprinkle cinnamon powder and sugar on top, if desired. Serve and enjoy warm!

Banana Cream Pie

Ingredients:

2 Fresh Bananas

3.4 oz. Banana Cream Pudding Mix

1 ½ cup Whole Milk

8 in. Graham Cracker Pie Crust (Ready Made)

¼ tsp. Vanilla Extract

½ tsp. Ground Cinnamon

8 oz. Cool Whip or Whip Cream

Instructions:

1. To begin, preheat the oven to 400°F. Once heated, bake the graham cracker crust for 10-12 minutes.
2. While the pie crust bakes, mix the banana cream pudding mix, whole milk, vanilla extract, and whisk until thickened, about 2-3 minutes. Add in ½ of the Cool Whip to mixture.
3. Remove from the pie crust from heat and allow to cool.
4. Slice the bananas into ¼ inch slices. Use the slices to evenly layer on the bottom of the crust.
5. Pour the cream mixture on top of the bananas, using a spoon to even out all sides.
6. Chill in refrigerator for at least one hour. Then add the remaining whip cream on top.
7. Sprinkle cinnamon lightly across the entire pie and serve. Enjoy!

Mouthwatering Oreo Milkshake

Ingredients:

3 cups All-purpose Flour

1 ½ cup Sugar

1 cup Butter, melted

1 Large Egg

1 ½ tsp. Vanilla Extract

1 ½ tsp. Ground Cinnamon

1 tsp. Baking Powder

¼ tsp. Sea Salt

Chocolate Syrup (optional)

Instructions:

1. To begin, place full oreos in a bag and use a meat mallet to gently crush into smaller pieces. Once crushed, set aside ⅓ cup to top the milkshake.

2. In a blender, add the following ingredients: whole milk, Vanilla Bean ice cream, and Cocoa powder. Blend until smooth and creamy.

3. Add in the oreos and continue to blend on a lower speed, so there are still crisp oreo pieces.

4. Before pouring the mixture into a cup, drizzle the chocolate syrup on the sides of the glass. Pour the mixture, top with whip cream and garnish with a reserved crushed oreos! Serve immediately and enjoy!

Sweet Apple Pancakes

Ingredients:

2 cups Fresh Apples (peeled, cored, and diced)
¾ cup Whole Milk
1 cup All-Purpose Flour
3 tbsp. Oil
1 Egg
1 tbsp. Vinegar
2 tsp. Ground Cinnamon
½ tsp. Baking Powder
½ tsp. Salt
3 tbsp. Powdered Sugar
3 tbsp. Brown Sugar
Fresh mint, for garnish

Instructions:

1. To begin, whisk the milk and vinegar together and allow to rest for 3-4 minutes. While resting, in a large mixing bowl add the following: flour, baking powder, salt, 1 tsp. Cinnamon, and brown sugar. Whisk together.

2. Add the egg and oil into the milk mixture and whisk again. Add the wet ingredients into the dry ingredients, as well as 1 ½ cups diced apple pieces. Mix well, but do not over mix as it should be lumpy.

3. Add cooking spray or 1 tbsp. Oil to a medium skillet, over medium-high heat. Pour ¼ cup pancake batter at a time and cook for about 1-2 minutes per side, until lightly golden. Repeat until all batter is gone.

4. To serve, place pancakes on a plate, sprinkle remaining ground cinnamon and powdered sugar on top. Garnish with fresh mint and enjoy hot!

Homemade Chocolate Mousse

Ingredients:

½-1 cup Semi-sweet Chocolate Chips

1 Cup Whole Milk

⅓ cup Chia Seeds

1 ½ cups Greek Yogurt, Plain

1 tsp. Vanilla Extract

1 ½ tsp. Honey

⅓ cup Shredded Coconut, for garnish

⅓ cup Cocoa Nibs, for garnish

Instructions:

1. To begin, in a medium saucepan over medium heat, heat the milk. Be careful not to let it boil. Once it is warm, begin stirring in the chocolate chips until melted and smooth.

2. Once melted, remove from heat and allow to cool for 5 minutes. Add in the chia seeds, honey, greek yogurt, and vanilla extract.

3. Pour into your desired ramekins or bowls and allow to chill in the refrigerator for at least 2 hours.

4. When ready to serve, remove from fridge and garnish with shredded coconut and cocoa nibs. Enjoy this chilly treat after a long day!

·THE·
SUPER MOM
Cookbook

Made in the USA
Lexington, KY
04 April 2019

·THE· SUPER MOM Cookbook

ISBN 9781942915799

9 781942 915799